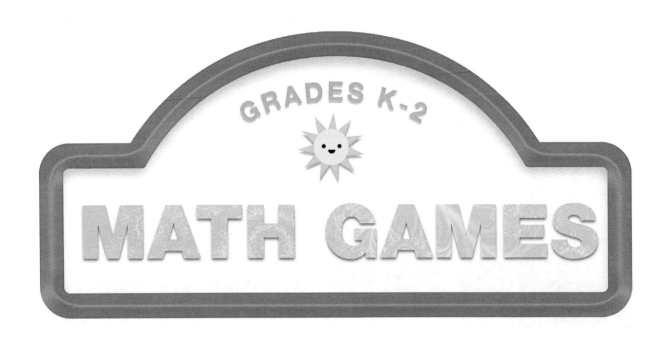

GRADES K-2

MATH GAMES

Glenview, Illinois • Boston, Massachusetts
Chandler, Arizona • Upper Saddle River, New Jersey

The Investigations curriculum was developed by TERC, Cambridge, MA.

This material is based on work supported by the National Science Foundation ("NSF") under Grant No.ESI-0095450. Any opinions, findings, and conclusions or recommendations expressed in this material are those of the author(s) and do not necessarily reflect the views of the National Science Foundation.

ISBN: 0-328-62645-7

ISBN: 978-0-328-62645-8

7 8 9 10 V0SV 17 16 15 14

Math Games K-2

Collect 20 Together Counting groups to 20	G1
Collect 25¢ Counting and trading coins	G2
Collect $1.00 Adding amounts to $1.00	G3
Compare Comparing numbers through 10	G4
Compare Dots Comparing numbers through 18	G5
Counters in a Cup Finding missing addends to 12	G6
Cover Up Finding missing addends to 45	G7
Dot Addition Making sums to 20	G8
Double Compare Dots Comparing sums through 20	G9
Fill the Hexagons Combining pattern blocks	G10
Five-in-a-row Subtraction Subtracting numbers from up to 12	G11
Get to 100 Adding multiples of 5	G12
Guess My Rule Sorting objects	G13
Heads and Tails Making sums to 12	G14
How Many am I Hiding? Finding missing addends to 12	G15
Make 10 Adding to make 10	G16
Make a Train Making repeating patterns	G17
Missing Numbers Finding missing numbers on a 100 chart	G19
Plus 9 or 10 Bingo Adding with 9 or 10	G20
Roll-a-Square Adding to fill 100 squares	G21
Roll and Record Adding to 12	G22
Ten Plus Finding equivalent sums	G23
Three Towers of Ten Making 10 in different ways	G24
Unroll-a-Square Subtracting to uncover 100 squares	G25
What's My Shape? Describing properties of solids	G26
Gameboards, Masters, and Recording Sheets	G27

Collect 20 Together

You need

- dot cube
- counters

Play with a partner. Work together.

1. Player 1 rolls the dot cube and takes that many counters.

2. Player 2 rolls the dot cube and takes that many counters.

3. After each turn, count how many counters you have.

4. Keep playing. Players work together to collect 20 counters.

5. The game is over when you have 20 counters together.

More Ways to Play

- Play with 2 dot cubes.
- Play with 1 dot cube and 1 number cube.
- Play *Collect 25 Together* or *Collect 30 Together*.
- Try to collect *exactly* 20 counters.

G1

Collect 25¢

You need

- dot cube or number cube

- coins

Play with a partner.

1 Player 1 rolls the cube and takes that amount in coins.

2 Player 2 rolls the cube and takes that amount in coins.

3 Keep taking turns. You can trade coins. At the end of each turn, figure out how much money you have.

4 The game is over when each player has collected at least 25¢.

More Ways to Play

- At the end of the game, try to make trades so that you have the fewest possible coins.
- Try to collect *exactly* 25¢.

Collect $1.00

You need

- two dot cubes  or number cubes

- money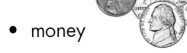

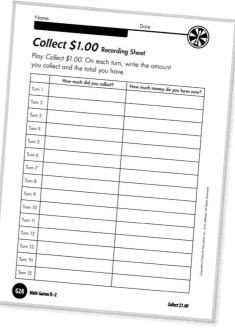

- recording sheet per player

Play with a partner.

1 Player 1 rolls the cubes, takes that amount in coins, and records the amount.

2 Player 2 rolls the cubes, takes that amount in coins, and records the amount.

3 Keep taking turns. You can trade coins. At the end of each turn, figure out how much money you have.

4 The game is over when each player has collected at least $1.00.

More Ways to Play

- At the end of each turn, try to make trades so that you have the fewest possible coins.
- Try to collect *exactly* $1.00.
- Play with a multiple-of-5 cube.
- Play *Collect $2.00.*

Compare

You need

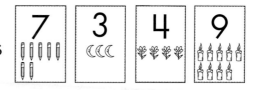

- deck of Primary Number Cards (without Wild Cards)

Play with a partner.

1. Deal the cards facedown.

2. Both players turn over the top card.

3. The player with the larger number says "Me!" and takes the cards. If the cards are the same, both players turn over another card.

4. Keep turning over cards. Each time, the player with the larger number says "Me!" and takes the cards.

5. The game is over when there are no more cards to turn over.

More Ways to Play

- The player with the **smaller** number says "Me!"
- Play with 3 players.
- Play with the Wild Cards. A Wild Card can be any number.

Compare Dots

You need

- Dot Cards

Play with a partner.

1. Deal the cards facedown.

2. Both players turn over the top card.

3. The player with more dots says "Me!" and takes the cards. If the cards are the same, each player turns over another card.

4. Keep turning over cards. Each time, the player with more dots says "Me!" and takes the cards.

5. The game is over when there are no more cards to turn over.

More Ways to Play

- The player with **fewer** dots says "Me!"
- Play with 3 players.

Counters in a Cup

You need

- 8–12 counters

- cup

- recording sheet

Play with a partner.

1 Decide how many counters to play with. Both players write this number on their recording sheets.

2 Count out that many counters.

3 Player 1 hides some of the counters under a cup.

4 Player 2 tells how many are hidden.

5 Player 1 removes the cup.

6 Both players count the counters that were under the cup and record that number.

7 Keep playing with the same set of counters. Take turns being Player 1 and Player 2.

8 The game is over when the grid is full.

Cover Up

You need

- 45 counters
- recording sheet per player

Play with a partner.

1 Decide how many counters to play with. Both players write this number on the recording sheets.

2 Count out that many counters.

3 Player 1 hides some of the counters under a piece of paper.

4 Player 2 tells how many counters are hidden.

5 Player 1 removes the paper.

6 Both players count how many counters were hidden and record that number.

7 Keep playing with the same number of counters. Take turns being Player 1 and Player 2.

8 The game is over when the recording sheet is full.

More Ways to Play

- Play with stickers.
- During Step 3, Player 1 *adds* some counters instead of hiding some. Player 2 figures out how many counters Player 1 added.

Recording Sheet (shown in illustration)

Name _____ Date _____

Cover Up Recording Sheet

Choose a total number. Count out that many objects. Player 1 hides some of the objects. Player 2 figures out how many are hidden.

Total Number	Number Not Covered	Number Covered

G34 Math Games K–2   Cover Up

G7

Dot Addition

You need

- deck of Dot Addition Cards

- 3 gameboards (one per player and one to play on)

Play with a partner.

1. Deal 4 rows of 5 cards, with the dots facing up.

2. Player 1 finds cards that combine to make one of the numbers on the gameboard.

3. Both players record the combination.

4. Player 2 finds cards that combine to make another number on the gameboard.

5. Both players record the combination.

6. The game is over when the gameboard is full.

More Ways to Play

- Play with different gameboards.

- Use each card only once.

- Play again, with the same gameboard. Try to find a different way to make each number.

Double Compare Dots

You need

- Dot Cards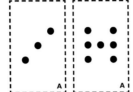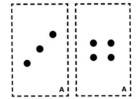

Play with a partner.

1 Deal the cards facedown.

2 Both players turn over their top two cards.

3 The player whose cards have more dots says "Me!" and takes the cards. If both pairs of cards have the same number of dots, both players turn over two more cards.

4 Keep turning over two cards. Each time, the player with more dots says "Me!" and takes the cards.

5 The game is over when there are no more cards in the deck.

More Ways to Play

- The player whose cards have **fewer** dots says "Me!"

- Play with 3 players.

Fill the Hexagons

You need

- pattern blocks
- 2 pattern block cubes
- gameboard (1 per player)

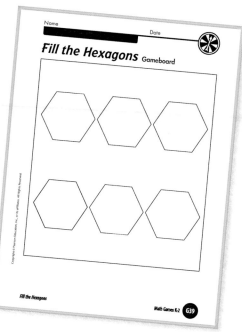

Play with a partner. Work together.

1 Player 1 rolls the pattern block cubes.

2 Player 1 places those pattern blocks anywhere on the gameboard. Once a block is placed, it cannot be moved.

3 Player 2 rolls the pattern block cubes.

4 Player 2 places those pattern blocks anywhere on the gameboard.

5 Players 1 and 2 continue playing, repeating steps 1–4.

6 The game is over when one player has covered all of the hexagons on the gameboard with blocks.

G10

Five-in-a-Row: Subtraction

You need

- 7–12 number cube
- dot cube
- 20 counters
- gameboard

Five-in-a-Row: Subtraction Gameboard

6	8	4	10	6
4	7	2	3	5
8	1	7	5	9
3	6	6	11	4
5	9	7	10	8

G40 Math Games K–2   Five-in-a-Row: Subtraction

Play with a partner. Work together.

1. Player 1 rolls two cubes.

2. Player 1 subtracts the smaller number from the larger number.

3. Player 1 covers that number on the gameboard.

4. Player 2 takes a turn, following steps 1–3.

5. If the number is already covered, roll again.

6. The game is over when all of the numbers in one row are covered. The numbers can go across ▢▢▢▢▢, down ▯, or corner to corner.

Get to 100

You need

- two multiple-of-5 cubes

- 100 chart

- game pieces

- recording sheet per player

Play with a partner.

1 Player 1 rolls two multiple-of-5 cubes and adds the results.

2 Player 1 moves a game piece that many spaces on the 100 chart.

3 Player 1 records.

4 Player 2 takes a turn and follows Steps 1–3.

5 Keep taking turns. On each turn, follow Steps 1–3.

6 The game is over when both game pieces reach 100.

7 Add the numbers on your recording sheet to make sure that they equal 100.

More Ways to Play

- Play on a number line.
- Play *Get to 200*. Use two 100 charts.
- Play *Get to 0*. Both players start at 100 and move backward the number of spaces rolled.

Guess My Rule

You need

- 20–25 buttons

- sorting mats

Play with a group of 2-4 players.

1. Player 1 chooses a rule that fits some of the buttons and writes it on a piece of paper.

2. Player 1 puts two buttons that fit the rule on the "These Fit My Rule" paper and two buttons that don't fit the rule on the "These Don't Fit My Rule" paper.

3. Player 2 puts a button where he or she thinks it belongs.

4. Players take turns placing buttons.

5. After each player has placed 3 buttons, players may try to guess the rule on their next turn.

6. The game is over once the rule has been guessed correctly.

7. Play again. Another player chooses the rule.

Heads and Tails

You need

- 8–12 pennies

- recording sheet

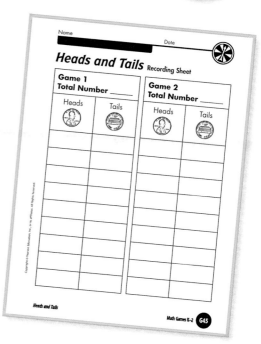

Play alone.

1 Decide how many pennies to play with. Record this number on the recording sheet.

2 Drop the pennies.

3 Count how many pennies are heads 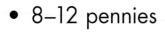 and how many pennies are tails .

4 Record the two numbers on the recording sheet.

5 Keep dropping the pennies and recording how they land.

6 The game is over when the grid is full.

How Many Am 1 Hiding?

You need

- 8–12 connecting cubes
- recording sheet

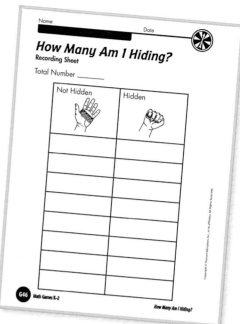

Play with a partner.

1. Decide how many cubes to play with. Both players write this number on their recording sheets.

2. Make a tower with that many cubes.

3. Player 1 hides some of the cubes.

4. Player 2 tells how many cubes are hidden.

5. Player 1 shows the hidden cubes.

6. Both players count how many were hidden and then record that number on their recording sheets.

7. Keep playing with the same tower. Take turns being Player 1 and Player 2.

8. The game is over when the grid is full.

More Ways to Play

- Play with 5 cubes of one color and 5 cubes of another color.

Make 10

You need

- deck of Primary Number Cards (without Wild Cards)

- blank sheet of paper

| 7 | 4 | 2 | 8 |

Play with a partner.

1. Deal 4 rows of 5 cards, with the numbers showing.

2. Player 1 finds two cards that make 10. Player 1 takes the cards and records the combination of 10.

3. Replace the missing cards with 2 cards from the deck.

4. Player 2 finds two cards that make 10. Player 2 takes the cards and records the combination of 10.

5. Replace the missing cards.

6. Keep taking turns finding two cards that make 10 and recording.

7. The game is over when there are no more cards or there are no more cards that make 10.

More Ways to Play

- Play with the Wild Cards. A Wild Card can be any number.
- Replace the cards *only* when there are no more pairs that make 10.
- Find more than 2 cards that make 10.

Make a Train (page 1 of 2)

You need

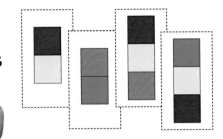

- *Make a Train* cards

- Color Cube

- connecting cubes

- a bag

- sheet of paper (or paper plate or a box) to be the "depot"

Play with a partner.

1. Each player draws a *Make a Train* card from the bag. Players use connecting cubes to make what is on the card.

   If Player 1 draws a red-yellow *Make a Train* card, he or she makes a car with a red cube and a yellow cube.

   If Player 2 draws a red-green-yellow *Make a Train* card, he or she makes a red-green-yellow car with those colored cubes.

Make a Train (page 2 of 2)

2 Player 1 rolls the Color Cube.

If the color rolled matches a color on either of the two trains, Player 1 takes a cube of that color and puts it in the "depot" (piece of paper, paper plate, or box). The depot is where the cubes are held until they can be made into cars.

If a star is rolled, the player can take any color.

If the color rolled is not in either of the two trains, the same player rolls again.

3 Player 2 rolls the Color Cube and places a cube of that color in the depot if either train has that color. The players check to see whether a complete car can be made for either train from the cubes in the depot.

4 Players continue to take turns and work together to make both trains 12 cubes long.

5 The game is over when there are two trains that are 12 cubes long.

Missing Numbers

You need

1	2	3	4	5	6	7	8	9	10
11	12	13	14	15	16	17	18	19	20
21	22	23	24	25	26	27	28	29	30
31	32	33	34	35	36	37	38	39	40
41	42	43	44	45	46	47	48	49	50
51	52	53	54	55	56	57	58	59	60
61	62	63	64	65	66	67	68	69	70
71	72	73	74	75	76	77	78	79	80
81	82	83	84	85	86	87	88	89	90
91	92	93	94	95	96	97	98	99	100

- 100 chart

- 10 pennies

- recording sheet

Name _____ **Date** _____

Missing Numbers Recording Sheet

Round 1: I think these numbers are missing.

_____ _____ _____ _____ _____

Round 2: I think these numbers are missing.

_____ _____ _____ _____ _____

Round 3: I think these numbers are missing.

_____ _____ _____ _____ _____

Round 4: I think these numbers are missing.

_____ _____ _____ _____ _____

Missing Numbers

Math Games K–2 **G47**

Play with a partner.

1. Player 1 covers five numbers on the 100 chart with pennies.

2. Player 2 figures out which numbers are missing.

3. Both players record the missing numbers on their recording sheets.

4. Remove the pennies. Check your work.

5. Take turns hiding the numbers.

6. The game is over when the recording sheet is full.

More Ways to Play

- Cover 10 more numbers.
- Play with a small group.

Plus 9 or 10 BINGO

You need

- deck of Primary Number Cards (without Wild Cards)

- two kinds of counters (20 per player)

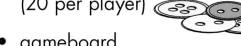

- gameboard

Plus 9 or 10 BINGO Gameboard

9	10	11	12	13	14
15	16	17	18	19	20
20	19	18	17	16	15
14	13	12	11	10	9
9	10	11	12	13	14
15	16	17	18	19	20

G48 Math Games K–2

Plus 9 or 10 BINGO

Play with a partner.

1. Player 1 turns over the top card in the deck.

2. Player 1 adds 9 or 10 to that number, and covers the sum on the gameboard.

3. Player 2 turns over the top card.

4. Player 2 adds 9 or 10 to that number, and covers the sum on the gameboard.

5. Keep taking turns. If all of the possible sums are covered, take another card.

6. The game is over when all of the numbers in one row are covered. The numbers can go across ⬜⬜⬜⬜⬜⬜, down ⬜, or corner to corner. ⬜

More Ways to Play

- Play with the Wild Cards. A Wild Card can be any number.
- Play to fill more than one row.
- Play as a team. Try to fill the entire gameboard.

G20

Roll-a-Square

You need

- two dot cubes  or number cubes

- 100 connecting cubes

- gameboard

Play with a partner. Work together.

1 Player 1 rolls and puts that many cubes snapped together on the gameboard. A row can only have 10 cubes. If cubes are left over, start a new row.

2 Player 1 looks under the last cube and follows the directions or answers the question on that square.

3 Player 1 says how many cubes there are in all.

4 Player 2 rolls and puts that many cubes on the gameboard. Remember, a row can only have 10 cubes. If cubes are left over, start a new row.

5 Player 2 looks under the last cube and follows the directions or answers the question on that square.

6 Player 2 says how many cubes there are in all.

7 Keep taking turns. The game is over when the gameboard is full.

More Ways to Play

- Play on Gameboard 2.
- Design your own gameboard.

G21

Roll and Record

You need

- 2 dot cubes
- recording sheet

Play alone.

1. Roll 2 cubes.

2. Add the numbers. +

3. Write the sum on the recording sheet.

4. The game is over when one column is full.

More Ways to Play

- Play with 1 dot cube and 1 number cube. **6**
- Play with 2 number cubes. **5** **4**

Ten Plus

You need

- deck of Primary Number Cards (without Wild Cards)

- 20 cubes

- recording sheet

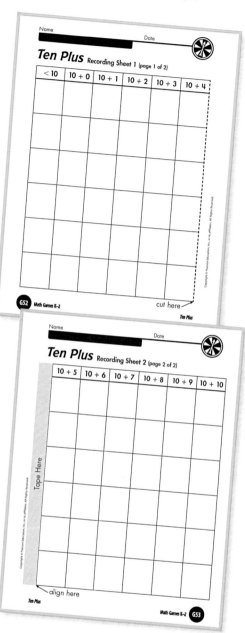

Play with a partner.

1 Turn over the top two cards.

2 Make an equivalent expression, using the two numbers from the cards and 10.

5 + 8 = 10 + ☐

3 Both players record 5 + 8 in the correct column on the recording sheet.

4 Turn over the next 2 cards and repeat steps 2–3.

5 The game is over when one column of the recording sheet is filled.

Three Towers of 10

You need

- dot cube

- 30 connecting cubes per player, in 2 colors

- crayons in 2 colors

- recording sheet

Play with a partner. Work together.

1. Each player picks a color of cubes.

2. Player 1 rolls and makes a tower with that many cubes.

3. Player 2 rolls and takes that many cubes.

4. Player 2 adds the cubes to the tower. A tower can have only 10 cubes. Start a new tower with any extra cubes.

5. The game is over when there are 3 towers of 10 cubes.

6. Both players record. Show how many cubes of each color there are in each tower. Write an equation for each tower.

More Ways to Play

- Make 5 towers of 10.
- Make 3 towers of 15.
- Play with 2 dot cubes.
- Play with 1 dot cube and 1 number cube.
- Play with 2 number cubes.

Unroll-a-Square

You need

- two dot cubes 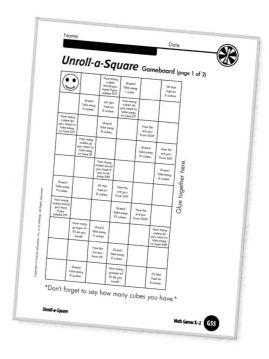 or

  number cubes

- 100 cubes

- gameboard

Play with a partner. Work together.

1 Place 10 cubes (snapped together) on each row of the gameboard.

2 Player 1 rolls and takes that many cubes off the gameboard.

3 Player 1 looks under the last cube and follows the directions or answers the question on that square.

4 Player 1 says how many cubes there are in all.

5 Player 2 rolls and takes that many cubes off the gameboard.

6 Player 2 looks under the last cube and follows the directions or answers the question on that square.

7 Player 2 says how many cubes there are in all.

8 Keep taking turns. The game is over when the gameboard is empty.

What's My Shape?

You need

- *Geometric Solids*

Play with a partner.

1 Choose a secret polyhedron (a shape with flat sides only) from the shapes on *Geometric Solids.*

2 Write the name of the polyhedron you chose on the back of this sheet or on another sheet of paper.

3 Write a description of the solid that will help someone guess the polyhedron you chose. Write at least two characteristics of your solid.

For example: My polyhedron has exactly 6 square faces and 8 corners. (My polyhedron is a cube.)

Gameboards, Masters, and Recording Sheets

	Page
Collect $1.00 Recording Sheet	**G28**
Dot Cards, Sets A-D	**G29**
Counters in a Cup Recording Sheet	**G33**
Cover Up Recording Sheet	**G34**
Dot Addition Gameboards	**G35**
Fill the Hexagons Gameboard	**G39**
Five-in-a-row: Subtraction Gameboard	**G40**
Get to 100 Recording Sheet	**G41**
100 Chart	**G42**
Guess My Rule Sorting Mats	**G43**
Heads and Tails Recording Sheet	**G45**
How Many Am I Hiding? Recording Sheet	**G46**
Missing Numbers Recording Sheet	**G47**
Plus 9 or 10 BINGO Gameboard	**G48**
Roll-a-Square Gameboards	**G49**
Roll and Record Recording Sheet	**G51**
Ten Plus Recording Sheets	**G52**
Three Towers of 10 Recording Sheet	**G54**
Unroll-a-Square Gameboards	**G55**

Collect $1.00 Recording Sheet

Play *Collect $1.00.* On each turn, write the amount you collect and the total you have.

	How much did you collect?	How much money do you have now?
Turn 1		
Turn 2		
Turn 3		
Turn 4		
Turn 5		
Turn 6		
Turn 7		
Turn 8		
Turn 9		
Turn 10		
Turn 11		
Turn 12		
Turn 13		
Turn 14		
Turn 15		

Name   Date

Dot Cards, Set A

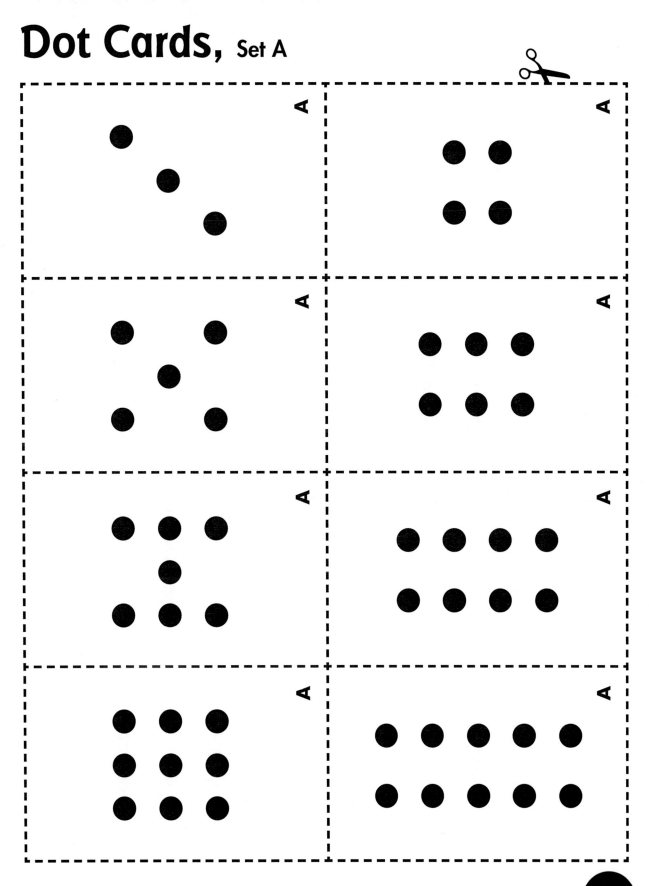

Compare Dots, Double Compare Dots   Math Games K–2   **G29**

Name

Date

Dot Cards, Set B

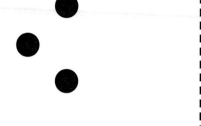 B

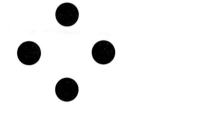 B

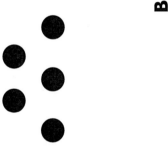 B

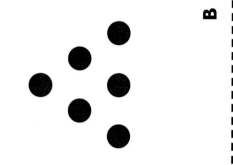 B

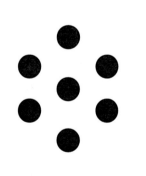 B

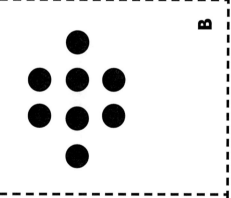 B

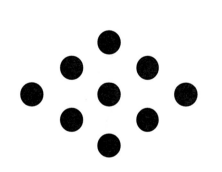 B

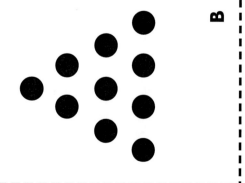 B

G30 Math Games K–2

Compare Dots, Double Compare Dots

Copyright © Pearson Education, Inc., or its affiliates. All Rights Reserved.

Dot Cards, Set C

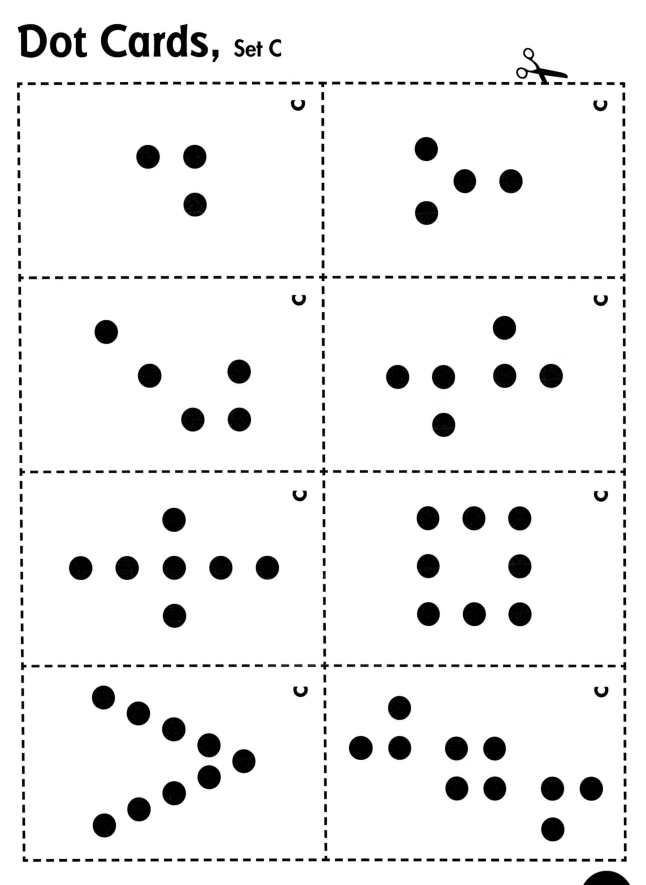

Compare Dots, Double Compare Dots

Dot Cards, Set D

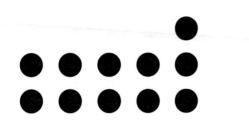 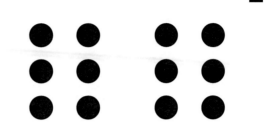

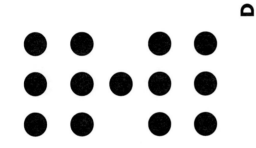 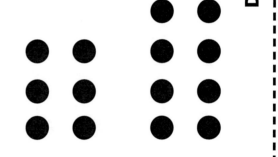

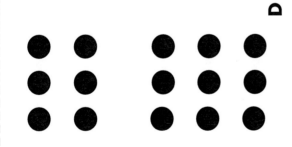 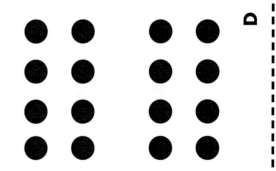

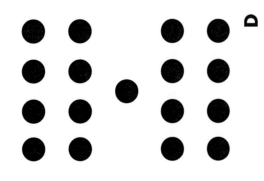 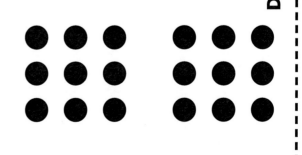

Counters in a Cup Recording Sheet

Total Number _____

Out	In

Cover Up Recording Sheet

Choose a total number. Count out that many objects. Player 1 hides some of the objects. Player 2 figures out how many are hidden.

Total Number	Number Not Covered	Number Covered
_____	_____	_____
_____	_____	_____
_____	_____	_____
_____	_____	_____
_____	_____	_____
_____	_____	_____
_____	_____	_____
_____	_____	_____
_____	_____	_____

Dot Addition Gameboard A

6
8
10
12

Dot Addition Gameboard B

6

9

10

15

Dot Addition Gameboard C

8
9
12
16

Name

Date

Dot Addition Blank Gameboard

Fill the Hexagons Gameboard

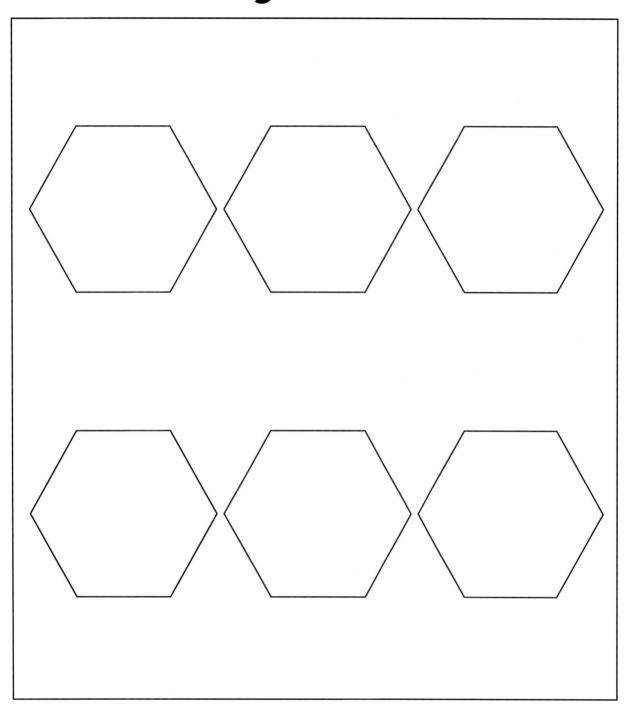

Name   Date

Five-in-a-Row: Subtraction Gameboard

6	8	4	10	6
4	7	2	3	5
8	1	7	5	9
3	6	6	11	4
5	9	7	10	8

Five-in-a-Row: Subtraction

Get to 100 Recording Sheet

Record each turn as you play. Only record the numbers rolled, not the total. When you get to 100 on the gameboard, show that your turns add to 100.

Game 1: I played this game with _____.

Game 2: I played this game with _____.

Name _____   Date _____

100 Chart

1	2	3	4	5	6	7	8	9	10
11	12	13	14	15	16	17	18	19	20
21	22	23	24	25	26	27	28	29	30
31	32	33	34	35	36	37	38	39	40
41	42	43	44	45	46	47	48	49	50
51	52	53	54	55	56	57	58	59	60
61	62	63	64	65	66	67	68	69	70
71	72	73	74	75	76	77	78	79	80
81	82	83	84	85	86	87	88	89	90
91	92	93	94	95	96	97	98	99	100

Name

Date

These Fit My Rule

These Don't Fit My Rule

Name _____ Date _____

Heads and Tails Recording Sheet

Game 1 Total Number _____		Game 2 Total Number _____	
Heads	Tails	Heads	Tails

How Many Am I Hiding?
Recording Sheet

Total Number _____

Not Hidden	Hidden

Missing Numbers Recording Sheet

Round 1: I think these numbers are missing.

_____   _____   _____   _____   _____

_____   _____   _____   _____   _____

Round 2: I think these numbers are missing.

_____   _____   _____   _____   _____

_____   _____   _____   _____   _____

Round 3: I think these numbers are missing.

_____   _____   _____   _____   _____

_____   _____   _____   _____   _____

Round 4: I think these numbers are missing.

_____   _____   _____   _____   _____

_____   _____   _____   _____   _____

Plus 9 or 10 BINGO Gameboard

9	**10**	**11**	**12**	**13**	**14**
15	**16**	**17**	**18**	**19**	**20**
20	**19**	**18**	**17**	**16**	**15**
14	**13**	**12**	**11**	**10**	**9**
9	**10**	**11**	**12**	**13**	**14**
15	**16**	**17**	**18**	**19**	**20**

Roll-a-Square Gameboard (page 1 of 2)

	Great! Take 12 more cubes.	How many more do you need to fill in this row of ten?			Oh No! Take away 3 cubes.
Great! Take 3 more cubes.		Oh No! Take away 6 cubes.	How far are you from 30?		
How many groups of 10 do you have?		Great! Take 6 more cubes.		How many more do you need to fill in this row of ten?	
	How far are you from 50?			Great! Take 5 more cubes.	How many more do you need to fill in this row of ten?
		How many groups of 10 do you have?			Great! Take 1 more cube.
Great! Take 7 more cubes.		Oh No! Give back 6 cubes.	How far are you from 70?		
How far are you from 80?		Great! Take 6 more cubes.		How many groups of 10 do you have?	
	How many more do you need to fill in this row of ten?				How many more cubes do you need to have 90?
		How far are you from 100?		Great! Take 9 more cubes.	
	Oh No! Give back 5 cubes.	How many more do you need to fill in this row of ten?			

Glue together here.

Don't forget to say how many cubes you have.

Roll-a-Square Gameboard (page 2 of 2)

How many more cubes do you need to have 20?		Oh No! Take away 2 cubes.	
Great! Take 1 more cube.	How many groups of 10 do you have?		Yes! Take 10 cubes.
		How many more cubes do you need to have 40?	
	Oh No! Give back 2 cubes.		How many more cubes do you need to have 70?
How far are you from 80?		Oh No! Give back 6 cubes.	Yes! Take 20 cubes.
	How many more cubes do you need to have 90?		
Oh No! Give back 6 cubes.		How many more do you need to fill in this row of ten?	
	Oh No! Give back 2 cubes.		How many groups of 10 do you have?
How many more do you need to fill in this row of ten?			Yikes! Give back 30 cubes.
	How many groups of 10 do you have?		☺

Name

Date

Roll and Record Recording Sheet

								12
								11
								10
								9
								8
								7
								6
								5
								4
								3
								2

Ten Plus Recording Sheet 1 (page 1 of 2)

< 10	10 + 0	10 + 1	10 + 2	10 + 3	10 + 4

cut here

Ten Plus

Ten Plus Recording Sheet 2 (page 2 of 2)

10 + 5	10 + 6	10 + 7	10 + 8	10 + 9	10 + 10

Tape Here

align here

Name

Date

Three Towers of 10 Recording Sheet

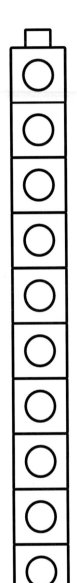  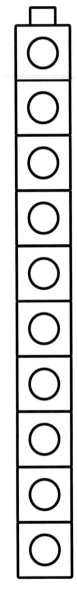

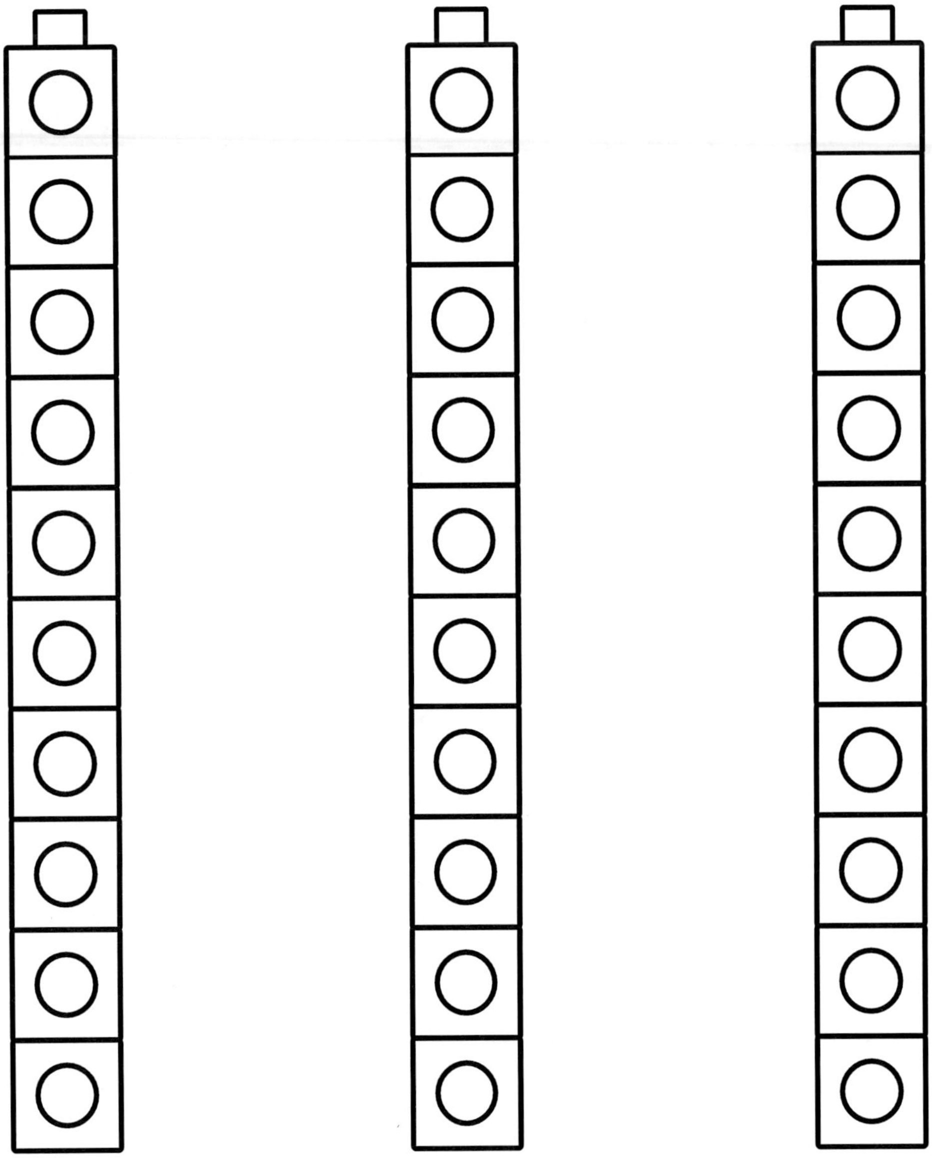

Equations

_____   _____   _____

Tower 1   Tower 2   Tower 3

Unroll-a-Square Gameboard (page 1 of 2)

☺		How many cubes would you have if you added 37?	Great! Take away 1 cube.		Oh No! Add on 5 cubes.
	Great! Take away 5 cubes.	Oh No! Add on 5 cubes.	How many cubes do you need to take away to have 0?		
How many cubes do you need to take away to have 10?		Great! Take away 9 cubes.		How far are you from 100?	
	How many cubes do you need to take away to have 2?			Great! Take away 6 cubes.	How far are you from 50?
		How many cubes would you have if you took away 23?			Great! Take away 3 cubes.
Great! Take away 11 cubes.		Oh No! Add on 8 cubes.	How far are you from 34?		
How many cubes would you have if you added 21?			Great! Take away 10 cubes.	How far are you from 100?	
	How many groups of 10 do you have?	Great! Take away 4 cubes.			How many cubes do you need to take away to have 56?
		How far are you from 0?	Great! Take away 5 cubes.		
	Great! Take away 5 cubes.		How many groups of 10 do you have?		Oh No! Add on 2 cubes.

Glue together here.

Don't forget to say how many cubes you have.

Unroll-a-Square Gameboard (page 2 of 2)

How far are you from 67?		Oh No! Add on 5 cubes.	
Great! Take away 10 cubes.	How many cubes would you have if you added 32?		Yikes! Add on 10 cubes.
		How many cubes do you need to take away to have 20?	
	Oh No! Add on 2 cubes.		How many groups of 10 do you have?
How many cubes do you need to take away to have 17?		Oh No! Add on 9 cubes.	Yes! Take away 10 cubes.
Great! Take away 3 cubes.	How many cubes would you have if you took away 10?		
Oh No! Add on 9 cubes.		How many cubes would you have if you took away 29?	
	Oh No! Give back 2 cubes.		How far are you from 10?
How many cubes would you have if you took away 30?			Yes! Take away 30 cubes.
	How many cubes do you need to take away to have 70?		